HORSE BREEDS

SHETLAND PONY

BY SAMANTHA S. BELL

Kids Core

An Imprint of Abdo Publishing
abdobooks.com

abdobooks.com

Published by Abdo Publishing, a division of ABDO, PO Box 398166, Minneapolis, Minnesota 55439.

Printed in the United States of America, North Mankato, Minnesota.
052025
092025

Cover Photo: Rita Kochmarjova/Shutterstock Images
Interior Photos: Shutterstock Images, 4–5, 10, 12–13, 23 (Clydesdale, Welsh, Shetland), 23 (Arabian), 28; Joe Giddens/PA Images/Getty Images, 7; Rita Kochmarjova/Shutterstock Images, 8, 9, 20–21; James Hime/Shutterstock Images, 14; NCJ Archive/Mirrorpix/Getty Images, 16; Kit Houghton/The Image Bank Unreleased/Getty Images, 18; C.Slawik/Juniors Bildarchiv GmbH/Alamy, 25; YAY Media AS/Alamy, 26; F368/Juniors Bildarchiv GmbH/Alamy, 29

Editor: Marie Pearson
Series Designer: Ryan Gale

Library of Congress Control Number: 2024949011

Publisher's Cataloging-in-Publication Data

Names: Bell, Samantha S., author.
Title: Shetland pony / by Samantha S. Bell
Description: Minneapolis, Minnesota: Abdo Publishing, 2026 | Series: Horse breeds | Includes online resources and index.
Identifiers: ISBN 9781098297510 (lib. bdg.) | ISBN 9798384930037 (ebook)
Subjects: LCSH: Shetland Pony--Juvenile literature. | Ponies--Juvenile literature. | Horse breeds--Juvenile literature. | Zoology--Juvenile literature.
Classification: DDC 636.16--dc23

CONTENTS

Some children's first ponies are Shetland ponies.

CHAPTER 1

A PERFECT MATCH

Allison and her dad pulled into the driveway of a pony farm. Allison could hardly wait. She and her dad were meeting a pony today. Her dad said it was a Shetland pony. If Allison liked it, it would become her very own!

Allison felt a little nervous. She had ridden several horses at her lesson barn. Some were tall and hard for her to mount. Some had a lot of energy and moved quickly. She wondered what this pony would be like.

As Allison and her dad walked toward the barn, a woman came out to meet them. She was leading a small brown-and-white pony with a thick mane and tail. Allison thought he was beautiful.

The pony nuzzled Allison's hand as she patted his nose. He waited patiently while she pulled herself into the saddle. Allison smiled as she felt her nerves melt away. She knew this gentle pony was just the right one for her.

A Shetland pony can typically carry up to 90 pounds (41 kg).

The Shetland pony, *right*, is much shorter than a horse, *left*.

Small but Mighty

Shetland ponies are the strongest type of horse for their size. But even the **stallions** are calm. Ponies and horses belong to the same species. But ponies are smaller than horses. Both horses

Like horses, Shetland ponies need time to run outdoors.

and ponies are measured in hands from the ground to the **withers**. One hand equals 4 inches (10 cm). A horse is taller than 14.2 hands. A pony measures up to 14.2 hands.

Why Hands?

People may have measured horses in hands in ancient Greece and Rome. It became the standard way to measure horses during the Middle Ages. A hand is the distance between a person's thumb and outstretched fingers. For the average hand, this distance is about 4 inches (10 cm).

Small children can ride Shetland ponies.

The Shetland pony's small size and strong build make it a good choice for a young rider's first pony. These ponies are also good partners for pulling carts or other activities. Their gentle nature makes them a favorite among both children and adults.

Explore Online

Look at the website below. Does it give any new information about Shetland ponies that wasn't included in Chapter One?

Shetland Pony

abdocorelibrary.com/shetland-pony

Wild Shetland ponies need thick fur to keep them warm.

HISTORY OF THE SHETLAND PONY

The Shetland pony originated on the Shetland Islands off the northern coast of Scotland. Over time, the ponies changed to **adapt** to their environment. The **climate** on the island is often harsh.

Shetland ponies still pull carts today. They can compete in a sport called driving.

Throughout the year, strong winds blow in from the sea. Because of this, the ponies developed shaggy, warm coats.

Much of the inland area of the island is made up of rocky hills. It is also covered by **peatlands**.

As the Shetland ponies roamed the hills and peatlands, they became tougher and stronger. Without many **nutritious** food sources, they also became smaller.

Around 850 CE, Vikings invaded Shetland. They settled on the islands and ruled them for about 600 years. The Vikings brought other ponies with them. These bred with the ponies on the island, creating the modern Shetland pony.

Work Horses

People who lived on the islands used the ponies to help them on their farms. The ponies were strong, and they could pull plows and other farm tools. The ponies were also used to move heavy loads.

Ponies that worked in mines were called pit ponies.

In the 1800s, coal mining became an important industry in Great Britain. People discovered that the small ponies were the right size for working in mines. They could easily pass through the tunnels. Miners used the ponies to haul the coal in coal cars. In the late 1800s,

Shetland ponies were brought to the United States to be used in coal mines there too.

By the mid-1900s, miners began using machines to move coal. The ponies were no longer needed. Some people in the United States began breeding the ponies for certain traits. They developed a breed called the American Shetland pony.

Pit Ponies

Some ponies had a hard time going into the mines every day. They became stressed traveling from the bright outside world to the dark mines. For this reason, most pit ponies were kept in stables down in the mines. Some spent most of their lives underground.

The American Shetland pony is taller and less stocky than the Scottish Shetland pony.

This breed is known for its gracefulness and performance. Today, both the Scottish Shetland and the American Shetland are admired for their unique traits.

Catherine Munro lives in Shetland. She explained how the islands shaped the Shetland pony:

> The characteristics that allowed ponies to live well on Shetland's wild [hills] are all [desired] traits today. Hardiness and adaptability means they can be happy in different environments, living in places other breeds would find difficult.

Source: Catherine Munro. "Shetland Ponies." *NorthLink Ferries*, n.d., northlinkferries.co.uk. Accessed 2 Oct. 2024.

Point of View

What is the author's point of view on Shetland ponies? What is your point of view? Write a short paragraph comparing the points of view. How are they similar? How are they different?

Some people breed Shetland ponies. They raise the foals.

LIVING WITH THE SHETLAND PONY

The Shetland pony is one of the most popular pony breeds in the world. About 1,500 Shetland ponies still live on the Scottish islands. Many are wild. They roam freely along the beaches and in the countryside.

These ponies have short legs, shaggy fur, and thick necks.

About 40,000 American Shetland ponies live in the United States. They are bred for certain traits. Some American Shetlands look like the ponies from the Shetland Islands. Other American Shetlands are taller. They have beautiful features and movement. They can have a lot of energy and high, showy **leg action**.

Even though there are different types of Shetland ponies, they all share some similar traits. For example, all Shetland ponies are small. Scottish Shetlands grow up to 10.2 hands tall. American Shetlands can grow up to 11.2 hands tall. Shetland ponies can be any color,

Shetland Pony Height

Shetland ponies are small for their species. They are also smaller than some other ponies.

but the most common colors are black and dark brown. Some Shetlands are white with patches of color.

Pets and Performers

Shetland ponies fill many roles today. Some are kept as pets because of their easygoing nature. They make good companions for people or for other horses. Children can learn how to ride and take care of them. Some Shetland ponies are even trained to help people as guide horses or service animals.

Racing for a Cause

The Shetland Pony Grand National is a team of Shetland ponies and riders in the United Kingdom. They race to raise money for charity. Riders must be 8 to 14 years old and under 5 feet (1.5 m) tall. The races are known for their fun, fast-paced atmosphere.

Some kids compete in jumping contests with their Shetland ponies. They follow a numbered course of jumps.

Many people enter their Shetland ponies in competitions. Kids can compete in pony hunter contests. As they ride their ponies, the ponies are judged on appearance, movement, and jumping ability.

Shetland ponies can make loving companions.

Adults can enter Shetland ponies in driving events. In these contests, the ponies pull carriages through a series of obstacles. Drivers must guide their ponies through the course.

Shetland ponies can be stubborn. Some may be challenging to train. But they are also friendly and even-tempered. Their playful personalities make them a good choice for children, adults, and families.

Further Evidence

Look at the article below. Does it give any new evidence to support Chapter Three?

Healing Hooves

abdocorelibrary.com/shetland-pony

BREED TRAITS

Broad head

Thick mane and tail

Thick neck

Short legs

American Shetland pony

Taller

Longer, thinner legs

Glossary

adapt
to change to become a better fit for an environment

climate
the usual weather in an area over a long period of time

leg action
the movement of a horse's legs when it walks, trots, or runs

nutritious
having substances the body needs to stay strong and healthy

peatlands
areas of wet ground where dead plants turn into a thick, soil-like substance called peat

stallions
male horses who can have offspring

withers
the highest part of a horse's back, located between its shoulder blades

Online Resources

To learn more about Shetland ponies and other horses, visit our free resource websites below.

Visit **abdocorelibrary.com** or scan this QR code for free Common Core resources for teachers and students, including vetted activities, multimedia, and booklinks, for deeper subject comprehension.

Visit **abdobooklinks.com** or scan this QR code for free additional online weblinks for further learning. These links are routinely monitored and updated to provide the most current information available.

Learn More

Barder, Gemma. *Be a Horse and Pony Expert.* Crabtree, 2021.

My Book of Horses and Ponies. DK, 2024.

Ventura, Marne. *Horses.* Abdo, 2023.

Index

About the Author

Samantha S. Bell lives in the foothills of the Blue Ridge Mountains with her family and four cats. She has written more than 150 nonfiction books for students from kindergarten through high school. She grew up around horses and ponies and sometimes rode them bareback.